"This book is brutal and bruta[...] addictive because Brontez Pur[...] [p]erformer in the truest sense. Reading *Ten Bridges I've Burnt*, I felt tucked in with him, along for the intimate ride, and I paused only once—to write down a part I'd been looking for my whole life."

—Miranda July, author of *The First Bad Man*

"This memoir in verse makes me enormously happy. To the things I know about Brontez Purnell add astral poet (in terms of imagination and scale) and classicist (elegant concerns). Witness it here. Lines leap out of themselves like light eruptions from the funniest angel you've ever seen. I could listen to this poet for hours, drive for days on a single thought: 'In my defense / I just had to signify / that poetry / is still dangerous.'"   —Eileen Myles, author of *a "Working Life"*

"I have been a fan of Brontez Purnell since I first saw him skipping gaily through San Francisco's streets in an early 2000s Younger Lovers video, and since then I've watched with pleasure as he's shared with the wider world his numerous talents as a performance artist, a fiction and nonfiction writer, a curator, and, not least, a lyricist and poet. *Ten Bridges I've Burnt* is Purnell's first collection of poetry, and it crackles like a live wire with his unique voice: Black, playful, gay, Southern, militant, joyful, queer, sexy, real, Bay Arean, and indisputably his own. Providing glimpses of the exciting life he's lived, *Ten Bridges I've Burnt* also suggests options for how to live in the world now."

—John Keene, author of *Punks: New & Selected Poems*, winner of the 2022 National Book Award for Poetry

"Brontez Purnell has impeccable comic timing and the gift of absolute candor. His poems leap off the page with insouciant, revolutionary speed. The urgent messages they deliver—with stinging wit and carefully honed critical defiance—provide inspiring models for how to perform, how to thrive, and how to write."   —Wayne Koestenbaum, author of *Ultramarine*

"In *Ten Bridges I've Burnt*, Brontez Purnell's language—bitchy, magnetic, dick-rich—is propulsive. His verse ladders down, alive with clear-eyed anger, bittersweet refusals. The braiding of emotions is jaw-dropping. One moment you're seething. The next, you're cackling. Defiant and timely, this book razes expectations, blazes in the mind long after you've finished it."

—Eduardo C. Corral, author of *Guillotine*, winner of the 2021 Lambda Literary Award for Gay Poetry and long-listed for the 2020 National Book Award for Poetry

"Written against the sanitized aesthetics of decorous poetry, Brontez Purnell's no-holds-barred collection, *Ten Bridges I've Burnt*, is an unapologetic—and always thrilling—romp through jizz, poetry fights, daddy (issues), coke, sex for money, and boyfriends of every race. In verse that is at once hard-edged, punk, and nakedly direct, Purnell refuses the terms of dour trauma porn in favor of playful irreverence, even as the poems go deep into the pain of life under heteropatriarchal racial capitalism."

—Jackie Wang, author of *Alien Daughters Walk into the Sun*

"Brontez Purnell's *Ten Bridges I've Burnt* is proof that 'poetry / is still dangerous.' It's a burn book / love letter to the Bay Area's queer demimonde. This book pushes back and forth in time, stopping to mop up at the Lusty Lady (RIP) before jogging around Lake Merritt. This is the memoir of an artist who helped queercore find its roots. If you read *Fag School* or sang along to "Danny," you're pulling gray hairs now. Purnell snatches the sting out of the words 'aging Black punk.' Thank god!"

—Cyrée Jarelle Johnson, author of *Slingshot*, winner of the 2020 Lambda Literary Award for Gay Poetry

Melissa Dale Neal

BRONTEZ PURNELL

TEN BRIDGES I'VE BURNT

Brontez Purnell is the author of several books, including *100 Boyfriends*, which won the 2022 Lambda Literary Award for Gay Fiction, was long-listed for the 2022 Mark Twain American Voice in Literature Award and the 2021 Brooklyn Public Library Literary Prize, and was named an Editors' Choice by *The New York Times Book Review*. The recipient of a 2018 Whiting Award for Fiction and the 2022 Foundation for Contemporary Arts Robert Rauschenberg Award, he was named one of the thirty-two Black Male Writers of Our Time by *T: The New York Times Style Magazine* in 2018. Purnell is also the frontman of the band the Younger Lovers and a renowned performance artist and zine-maker. Born in Triana, Alabama, he has lived in Oakland, California, for two decades.

Also by Brontez Purnell

100 Boyfriends

The Nightlife of Jacuzzi Gaskett
(illustrated by Elise R. Peterson)

Since I Laid My Burden Down

Johnny Would You Love Me If My Dick Were Bigger

TEN BRIDGES I'VE BURNT

MCD Farrar, Straus and Giroux   New York

TEN BRIDGES

I'VE BURNT

A MEMOIR IN VERSE

BRONTEZ PURNELL

MCD
Farrar, Straus and Giroux
120 Broadway, New York 10271

Printed in the United States of America
First edition, 2024

Title-page art by Na Kim.

Emoji on page 106 designed by OpenMoji—the open-source emoji and
icon project. License: CC BY-SA 4.0.

Library of Congress Cataloging-in-Publication Data
Names: Purnell, Brontez, author.
Title: Ten bridges I've burnt: a memoir in verse / Brontez Purnell.
Description: First edition. | New York: MCD / Farrar, Straus and Giroux, 2024.
Identifiers: LCCN 2023038964 | ISBN 9780374612696 (paperback)
Subjects: LCSH: Purnell, Brontez. | Poets, American—21st century—Biography. |
    LCGFT: Autobiographies. | Autobiographical poetry.
Classification: LCC PS3616.U785 Z46 2024 | DDC 813/.6 [B]—dc23/eng/20231004
LC record available at https://lccn.loc.gov/2023038964

Designed by Gretchen Achilles

Our books may be purchased in bulk for promotional, educational,
or business use. Please contact your local bookseller or the Macmillan
Corporate and Premium Sales Department at 1-800-221-7945, extension 5442,
or by email at MacmillanSpecialMarkets@macmillan.com.

www.mcdbooks.com • www.fsgbooks.com
Follow us on social media at @mcdbooks and @fsgbooks

10 9 8 7 6 5 4 3 2 1

To the one who burns bridges—
better be prepared to swim.

So I got kinda confused and I had to sit down to write this
   poem
The subject was faggots.

—GIL SCOTT-HERON, "The Subject Was Faggots"

But had I accepted the pickle juice, I would be drinking pickle
juice right now.

—NICKI MINAJ

Contents

TEN BRIDGES I'VE BURNT

Oath of Athenian Youth

I was born in Athens (Alabama)
this tells you nothing, but I will try.
Though it's named after
that great city
of antiquity
I know nothing of olive trees and oracles
only cotton stalks
and rivers poisoned with DDT
I cannot recite the oath of Athenian youth
I betray my birth city
it is not the oath in my heart
I am not the child of a god
nor of a senator
my father was once a soldier
and I
am a divine normal
my father labored
until he died
my mother
has labored
since my birth

Though born in Athens
I

ring truer
as a child of Sparta
I live in a Spartan hellhole (America)
our gods study war
subsequently
I am bloody

Up the road
sat a war city, Huntsville
Redstone Arsenal army base
the army base where my mother
a secretary
sat me by her side
and I watched the soldiers
dance with guns
and
march and chant
("I don't know, but I've been told . . .")

I was supposed to be a soldier one day
and I'd argue that maybe I am still
if only conceptually

I sat by my mother's side
listening to the soldiers
I forgot that these men were

instruments of death
(though in times of peace—maybe conceptually)
I guess I only saw a
chorus line
of very handsome
showgirls
generating a rhythm that I
a future daydreamer
would code

I look for rhythm
in everything:
a pen going across paper
feet hitting pavement
and my personal favorite
a room
of aimless chattering
but back to my city
I can't tell you much
about ancient Greece to be honest
except that I, an American,
have had the notion
shoved down my throat
that these white folks in the Fertile Crescent
were REALLY onto something
what with art and slave owning

and what have you
and so
I, a child of Athens,
need only to see
a bleached white marble column
and be reminded of home
and though I hate free association
every time
I see a bleached marble column
I see the Klansmen's hoods
I can like,
smell the cross burning
forgive me if this troubles YOU
I was a grown man in California
before I learned
that Africa too had gods
that could shoot lightning, start wars, inspire pathos,
    represent the elements
and like every other Black man
whose soul was switched
with that of a Greek boy's of antiquity
I often close my eyes
and try to picture Nigeria or Ghana
but remember
that I am only an African boy
conceptually

and when I complain I am reminded
by some
asshole
that people are starving
from Africa
to the Appalachians
and that suffering
does not make me special

Like every other American
I am only an echo
of the Old World
but I personally sometimes feel
that I am becoming and unbecoming
both louder and fainter
simultaneously and into infinity
and dear god
I am already so tired

"We will never bring disgrace to this, our city, by any act of
    dishonesty or cowardice"

And do I refuse this oath?
Do I have any sense of borders left?
My body, a sort of nation-state
the only city I have left

is the one inside
Where is the "Oath of Nowhere"?
I could easily
draw you a map
of where I was
born
and have it tell you
absolutely nothing
about me

Alumni Sweater

I graduated from UC Berkeley
the summer of '88
I am a crowning achievement of liberality
I often wear my Berkeley sweater some thirty years after
its relevance to me
near as I can tell
when the fabric clings to my perfect goddamn muscle daddy
     gym body
to the rest of the world
all my bullshit is rendered virtually scentless
it's a look that reads
"I fuck white boys and voted for Biden"

when I wear my Berkeley sweater in New York City
I read as a "pussy nigga"
and I literally can't deal
but
all in all
if I really had to think about it
I am indeed
very, very soft
and very, very warm
but all pussy talk aside

I'm still a nigga
still a threat
wanna bet?
I promise you
swear on my mother's life even
that when I wear my Berkeley sweater back home in Alabama
I read as an "outside agitator"
which even in Alabama still reads as
"he fucks white boys and voted for Biden"

they wrongly assume
like so many
that I made these choices
without weighted reflection
or they even credit me
with splitting the difference of the average mean
of general choices
a man in my situation is allowed

rarely does the path of least resistance
still not leave my fat ass sweating
and sometimes, very rudely,
it's not offered to me at all
I make this shit look seamless
because I'm good at it
and I'm very, very, very afraid not to

freshman year I took a Sociology 303 class
"Magic and Religion"
it described the "trickster"
as "both superhuman and subhuman"
again
I split the difference
because even when I'm telling the truth
I'm still always in disguise
beyond the static on my alumni sweater
sit the facts:
I am
a handsome Black man
with a fat ass
and a demonically expensive liberal arts education
that said
why do I
so often
stand in front of my bathroom mirror after washing my face
the third, fourth, fifth time
and think
"Who will save me from my fate"?

And I Am Serving Fuck Boy Like
It's Going Out of Style . . .

I'm so fuckin' over me
I can't even make myself hard for me anymore
every time I get my dick hard to masturbate
the voice in my head is like
"Ew, this guy again?"
It's a process.

Instead I go out walking after midnight
under streetlights
on avenues where any ol' body will do
now I laugh at the contradictions of myself—though a
    reasonable person would call these *boundaries*
I refuse to buy a butane-less lighter from a homeless man
    because I'm afraid I might catch a cold from his handshake
    yet I'd probably suck his dick if he asked nicely
I'm Amanda by night
but in the daytime on the street
I'm all fist bumps (no shook hands)
and I largely avoid eye contact
even in the straight Black boy barbershop
I use the only "straight man" voice I can muster: silence
I know my barber doesn't give a shit—he's an older man, he's

a Democrat, he's seen faggots before, and as said specimen
    I'm particularly not that remarkable
but
there is that old voice in my head that I can't ever shake: that
    if I make too much of a fuss
my fade will be less than tight
and I simply can't take that chance.

Is there such a thing as pre-traumatic stress syndrome?
I'm neat.
"The creases in my pants are so motherfucking sharp you
    could cut your goddamn hand on 'em" as my father once
    put it
I'm wearing a couture tailored flower-print dashiki cut from
    Japanese silk. There are roses drawn in abstract on the
    print
my little perfect chocolate nipples are rubbing up against the
    fabric
I'm wearing tight jeans
I walk like I wanna get fucked.

I wear Vans when I wanna fuck a white boy and Jordans when
    I wanna fuck a Black boy and vintage white Jordans when
    I really wanna stunt and fuck every boy in the fuckin'
    neighborhood
I'm wearing a Raiders cap and ghetto diamond earrings

I am serving "fuck boy" like it's going out of style
I am serving "fuck (me) boy" like it's going out of style.

To the untrained eye I look like I graduated from Hillman
    College
I look like the boy you would least suspect
when I walk down the street rest assured that I will not
    remember your name
but more importantly
rest assured
that you don't know me.

I'm Bloody by Nature,
Not 'Cause I Hate Ya

Of course, we should fear bad men . . .
"The gods need to eat today"
said the boy who shot sixteen of his classmates
said the man who hit his wife
said the man who jumped from a roof and fucked up some
    innocent person's car
I too am bloody
they often tell me so
this EGREGIOUS fucking honky piece of shit
was trying to fuck my wife
I was on cocaine
in a circle of strangers
ya'know, like, being myself
(ya'know, like, "how I am")
and when I left the circle
he was like
"Is that man always so bloody?"
my wife told me this
whilst lying in bed that night
and much like counting sheep I counted all the things I am as
    bloody as
one by one

jumping across a fence

I am as bloody as:

The Gaza Strip; Ferguson; Laura Palmer; bloodstones; blood oranges; blood brothers; a *Game of Thrones* episode; Pussy ("Do you need to change your sanitary napkin?" as my father would say, when I was "being a pussy"); Remy Ma vs. Nicki Minaj; Azealia Banks vs. literally fucking everybody; Money; *Mortal Kombat*; the boy who gave me HIV; the friend who publicly scandalized my name; the Blood Moon; Helter Skelter; the Manson Girls; George Zimmerman; Jeffrey Dahmer; Marielle Franco; the Iron Triangle; Any American President; Any American Soldier; *Roots* by Alex Haley; *All Eyez on Me* by Tupac Shakur; my mother; my father; my baby sister; my suicidal white girl roommate; a Sylvia Plath poem . . .

(I'm too tired to count sheep anymore . . .)

I insist that I am only as bloody as my memories.

Was it the joke I made about my stepfather?

Is this what offended the egregious honky bastard who
    wanted to fuck my wife?

Is that little statement what gassed that bitch?

I insist I could have said something bloodier.

But when considering the man I offended

I become more and more

uninspired

because to someone as bloodless as that man
I'm certain that someone like me
is as red-looking
as a packet of ketchup
though blood and ketchup are both red
and mostly made up
of complex sugars.

LOTTERY WINNER

"Despite all my bids to the contrary
I am still just a fussy old man
Who does not get his way very much
But this time
I think I shall . . .
Who are you?
I.
Will.
Eat.
You.
Up."

Guy-o-logical Clock: Ticking

I violently refute the unspoken cultural assumption
that I
a promiscuous gay man
and
toxic-ass bachelor
should etch "Unmarried and Childless"
on my tombstone
for I have been a damn good husband to myself
and have spent my best years raising all my friends
yet also
have whittled time away in group therapy sessions
with a great many middle-aged men who are also in recovery
and are mad at forty
'cause their parents divorced when they were ten.

I try not to judge
but this reads as extravagant to me
that the lie of the nuclear family failed them
and I can't relate
my parents never married
and I had the privileged position
of being a pagan love child
my father, the asshole and the prophet

looked at me at seven and said
"Son, you were born doomed"
and honestly, "doomed" is just an easier place to operate
    from.

My willful optimism has always operated on the belief that
    the show must go on
I cry with these men
though also show restraint
out of respect for the friends I've raised
who had neither a latch nor a key
but I also share in the sentiment
that if something had been better in the past
I might be better in the present too?
At this point it means nothing
but as of late
I do admit the weakness
of fearing the fatherhood that eludes me
too often the same dream
of a baby
sleeping on my chest
and I awaken thinking
"Something is missing?"
I look to the left and right
but quickly remember

there has only ever been me here
and so it goes.

As I watch my own effacement
the lines in my face grow numerous
and the hair keeps graying and falling out
and my midlife crisis
is the opposite of most men's
I am only following the law of the universe that
everything
eventually cools
to the temperature around it
though all in all
my guy-o-logical clock
has been newly set to ticking
and well past my youth
my body remains a hand grenade.

NAKED COUSIN

I posted one pinche fuckin' picture
of a long-lost cousin
I didn't know I had
a perfect stranger
who doesn't look like me
but sharing the same last name
was permission enough
for every thirsty fucking faggot
to check up on this picture of my naked cousin
more than on me

I have suspected in parts
more people would fuck me
if I was someone else
less fat here
or more (depending on who you ask)
more eyelashes
or
more romance
maybe their attraction
was the comfort
of something familiar yet foreign enough
to not breed contempt

but my contempt stands
as does somewhat of a worse fear:
that nobody wants my body
but everyone wants my soul

Point Nemo

1.

When the weird sisters asked
"When shall we three meet again?
In thunder, lightning, or in rain?"
I know:
the poetics of the void notwithstanding
scientists wager to reason it
a pole of inaccessibility
but poetically
you could say
if the Earth were flat
it would be the ocean ledge
where one would fall off
though being plotted
in the pressurized circumference of the planet
does not make its exactitude
any more dimensional
all the spaceships are buried there
and though only reachable by water
no sailor has ever dared a journey to
"Nemo"
Latin for "no one"

2.

Oh honey, you know I'm terrible
at taking care of myself
and even when
I'm not depressed
or high on drugs
how easily
2:00 a.m. becomes 3:00 a.m.
becomes 5:58 a.m.
becomes sunrise
but at no point will you find me
caught beneath the landslide
I have been seasick
so long
it's become a pleasant feeling
I am a vertigo romantic
how special a feeling
where everyone tells me
my mind hallucinates
violent movement
in what is actually stillness
but I think honestly
I feel something deeper
I shit you not
I am the only one

who can actually feel the Earth
hurtling through space
yes, that must be it
the waves keep on crashing on me for some reason

3.

"I want more than what I'm worth"
is a sailor's prayer
roughly translated
and also
"If not tonight, the future"
and so on
"I'm a sailor on the ocean—I need nothing to keep going"
I say these things under my breath
at each transition I could
just as likely
be a bit less earnest about it
these mantras of course
are built in the hopes that I stay very close to the Earth
I maintain an ill-fated pact
with staying landlocked
when I could just as easily
leave my body behind
guilt free

not like death
but in other abstracts

I'm one of those people
who always wondered
what it would be like
to sucker punch a close friend
mid-conversation
or toss a drink in their face
for no other reason
than to see
what the effect would be upon impact but
in the spirit of self-preservation
I pray into existence
the geographic coordinates
where "leaving your body"
is an actual physical place you can go
and not
a perilous occupation

In consulting
the oracle
of oceanographers
who for all practical reasoning have found
the middle point
of the deepest nowhere

fatalistic me can only paint

in my mind

a waterbed of black waves

spanning every blurred horizon

I get a flushed feeling

of imagining

a coffin

I am terrified and suffocating

with fear

and panic

but if I reach a little deeper

or maybe to the left

I see

in other mythologies

a certain Zen

If I Had a Time Machine,
I Would Kill My Parents . . .

so goes the question
"what would you do if you had a time machine"
of course the only answer is
"kill my parents"
but I, being in the habit
of problematizing EVERY fucking thing,
want to kill the version of my parents
that is already dead
the people they were in the eighties
and even into the early nineties
I see my mother
wilting on the floor
exhausted
she doesn't raise hell with me anymore
not because of any great fear
but simply because
she doesn't have the energy
what we call "wisdom"
could easily be called "fading of hormonal response"
and oh it's fine
'cause now that I'm my parents' age
I understand it all too well

I have an anarchist friend
who laments that his mother
simply won't go to therapy
and that's bad
but I dare not say
that sitting in a room
with some white man
won't melt away
her sixty-plus
years
of muscle memory trauma
our parents defy therapy
unlike many of my generation
I'm actually sometimes silently impressed
at the level of asshole these people are
oh my poor father
all he wanted me
to do
was like pussy and shut the fuck up
I literally only had one job
or two
depending on how you look at it
I used to say
"why would I marry a woman just to disappoint her"
but honestly
my boyfriends tend to be disappointed too

and I don't fuck them either
all my father could see
was that I grew up with my own room with a color TV
a far cry
from him sharing bathwater with his nine siblings
"no, he's FINE"
and generationally
he's actually right
paired against what he knows of the world
my trauma reads as unremarkable to him
perhaps even "common"
"I'm the reason you're handsome"
is often how he ends a fight
of course he lets himself off the hook
and if I really had to deal with the predicament of
whose fault my childhood was
all I can say is
"it took a village"
speaking of which

back to the village empress
my mother
the feminist angst
of the seventies and eighties
said that women are more than allowed
to hate their husbands

and bosses
but how did children get off the hook so easily
hating your children
is perfectly feminist
we conclude the trifecta
of marriage house and imprisonment
true we didn't ask to be born
but that hardly holds up in court
'cause goddamn
if we didn't ask for everything else

my poor mother
all she wanted me to do
was shut the fuck up
she didn't even care
about me liking pussy
she just wanted me quiet
a child of divine silence
I recognize now
that in her heart buzzed a migraine
and women must always be tired
and I inherited
yet another feminine trait: exhaustion

I don't really need a time machine
as the Earth spinning is one

and being in the collapse of gravity
I too succumb to centrifugal force
the machine of time
will do this to all
and I join my mother on the floor oh the years
bloody noses and bones
screaming matches
melt to nothing
and submit to the laws of Earth and memory
that time pressure and erosion
decay everything
even perhaps my anger
and despite all refusal
we remain heroes

RAGE OF EVERY COLOR

You want to see me explode into colors, don't you?
If I could dream of every night and be so quick to silence it
annihilate each laid brick
of the house I retrofit
you deliberately misinterpret me, like, constantly
see me only as the man
who represents
the ten bridges I've burnt
but not the hundred that I've built
girl, fuck you
whether or not
multiplicity is
to your taste
I shall give you a feast

TOMMY CHIN

I had jumped Tommy Chin
at the San Francisco Young Gay Poets Luncheon
in 2004
because in my youth
I struggled with decorum
she had dissed my poetry
in the annual newsletter
which I would have forgiven if she had not also had the nerve
to be skinnier than me too
not that being skinnier than me is any great feat
yet still
that bitch had to die
oh the critique in her venomous post about me!
It rang to the tune of
"Well, why should we trust this voice"
MEANWHILE
her white-ass boyfriend
in the same poetry newsletter mind you
actually published
seven typed rows
of the lowercase *e*
and was praised
for his devotion
to space shape and time

first of fuckin' all

if I really think about it

that is the list
of who was both let into and shit all over
the club called "experimental literature"
why the fuck at this point
need we question
someone as pure as me
about ANY goddamn thing
and every time someone
who isn't a nigga
or jazz adjacent
critiques my work
with excessive force
I still basically smile and bear it
but can't turn off the emotional switch that
English, regrettably
is my only language
and I am being told, a little too often for my liking,
that I have no real command of it

if I am not writing
like someone's favorite dead white man
or even more insultingly

like someone's white-ass boyfriend
I had let these bitches
play me
like a pit bull
in a basement
for far too long
my bad mood
had started in the morning
I was young and kept late hours
and never smelled the fire burning
but on my way to the luncheon
the entire warehouse of the near-homeless
had burned
it was word on the street
the landlord had did it
and my hooker friend Chyna
was sick and standing on the corner and needed money for
    dope
and Tommy sat in an apartment in the Castro
with his poet boyfriend
and it occurred to me
that I had always been closer to being homeless
than I had ever been to living
with a boyfriend in the Castro
this was not Tommy's fault
but I guess I just got tired of feeling

like EVERY fault was mine?
But if I really think about it
this is not about race
this is not about class
this is about my ego vs. these other corny bitches
and sometimes
I take great pleasure
in reminding people who have hurt me
why I am stronger than them
"Tommy, my love, I want you to know that I hold space for
    and respect our mutual positionality as men of color in
    the sisterhood of battling white supremacy in the writing
    world"
is what I SHOULD'VE said
before I jumped him
but I was speechless
when I did a full-frontal tackle
and gripped his throat
his white-ass boyfriend
stayed all the way out of it

of course

and I thought it was a horrible racist trope
of like
Asian Americans
being proficient at martial arts and so I

almost never saw that right hook coming

that split my front right incisor in half

blood dripping from my gums

and he hit me again

and now I think I'm in love with him?

My choke hold lost its economy

and Tommy caught his breath

for all of three seconds

before he charged me

and in a moment of divine clarity

I mumbled

"I mutually give honor and respect to our positionality as
    men of color, Tommy"

right before I grabbed a glass pitcher and hit him in the head
    so hard that to this day

I am banned from the San Francisco Young Gay Poets
    Luncheon

but in my defense

I just had to signify

that poetry

is still dangerous

On Writing

1.

. . . I can be quite vexed about how much American
    audiences
overestimate
their grasp of plot
those godless bitches
are the WOOOOOOOOORST
somewhere
in the majority of collective consciousness
the notion of plot
is forever held hostage
by the introduction chapter of *Intro to Plot*
if I recall correctly
it reads:
"Synopsis: The killer is in the house, the car is outside, the car
    keys are SOMEWHERE, one must find the keys to get to the
    car, to escape the killer, AND THAT IS PLOT!"
I
being the total fatherless pussy that I am
am always wondering
about the emotional cracks
that lie within

this fictional narrative

the emotional landscape within the killer

him pondering that time he picked a flower in his youth

and was happy

before he slits

some screaming bitch's throat

or even

the car

like, how did the car feel?

Was it a wedding gift?

A Volvo?

I can reason

that every person

who has ever criticized literature

who dared utter "the plot was paper-thin"

had to look at the arc of their own lives

and

if they were being honest

said the same thing

I am

a TV writer

and can sit quite comfortable

in the continuous existential crisis

that if a room of twelve people

dissected the choices of my life

none of it would make sense
or they would conclude that
I have never once made
"the right choice"

I am
a TV writer
and am in the habit
of making problems
my producer corrected me
quite sincerely
over a nineteenth draft
of a thirteenth scene
I said to him "I needed these characters to have a resolution"
and he said
"THIS ISN'T A MOVIE. NETWORK TV IS NOT IN THE
    BUSINESS OF 'RESOLVING THINGS.' IF YOU HAVE A
    SOLUTION, YOU NO LONGER HAVE DRAMA—AND YOU
    SIR WILL BE OUT OF A JOB."
PROPHETIC WORDS.
I liken it
to the time I was a jizz mopper
at a strip club
in North Beach
and the madam told me
and the other fag there

"You can hook up with the guys but you CAN'T. MAKE.
     THEM. CUM. When they cum
they stop spending money"

2.

I am
the first son
of a third daughter
of a family of ten
in certain European folklores
I hold what is called a "cursed position"
subsequently
drama tends to surround me
so I decided to get paid for it.

I am
a TV writer (again a "cursed position")
I have joined every cult
ever offered to me
with VIGOR
I throw MYSELF to the wolves
I'm like that girl
in the gang bang videos
who lightly giggles "I'm nervous"

before clocking in to work
and oh my stars and garters
I don't actually even like TV
but also I am a master
of scripting unsolvable problems
for myself and for others
I like writing for TV
mostly because
I don't have to pretend anymore
that I'm not a drug addict
some writers really buy into that whole
"narrator as god" bullshit
in reality
I'm more a nanny
because it recently occurred to me
that I attend
to the personal well-being
of fictional characters
more than I do to my own
and drama follows me home
more often than I'd like to talk about
I have blacked out on GHB
in a random motel room
And have woken up to the vigorous shaking
of a hooker I hired for sex
"SIR, ARE YOU OK?!"

I think the poor guy
was alarmed
that they would find me dead
at a Days Inn in the Tenderloin
with traces of his semen
in my abdomen and rectum
and his fingerprints on my phone
where he tried to steal a thousand dollars
from my bank account
and again
I dosed myself
but like
isn't *the hooker* supposed to drug you?
If I drug myself—isn't it god's will that a hooker robs me?

These are all questions I pose in the writers' room
next to my coworkers whose lives I'm sure are just as
    fucked-up
but who have been doing it so long
that there is no real drama left in anything
"We actually have to concentrate now"
says the man to my left
and I'm reminded how I'm always starkly oversharing
but the truth sometimes
has this two-dimensionality
that I can't always fit

over my overly three-dimensional world
'cause I, my love,
am a pathological liar
I've done it so long
what other decent profession
would have me?

Saturday Day Night Blues

My rage smells like nostalgia
I am
a troubled Negro youth
in his forties
neglecting self-repair
and I am recoiling
the anger in my old man days
Is/As/Was
the anger of my youth: nobody cares and nobody believes me
    when I say something is hurting me
I left the fan on all day
hoping the white noise would carry me into sleep
but what would "black noise" even be?
In accordance with natural law, in an expanding and
    collapsing universe
I imagine the sound
of an infinite amount of little tears
so loud it's silent
a certain violence
I am accustomed to
every time my boss talks to me
be it praise or scorn
I notice I stop breathing

and later learn that animals who are heavily preyed upon
    will often stop their own breath
in an attempt
to hear their surroundings better
of course that sounds very likely
but also just can't be true
because too often in silence
I can't locate my heart beating
take it for granted
liken it to the fact
that I don't need to see my feet to know that they are there
round about and round about
who wants a life anyway?
He calls from rehab
on Tuesdays and Saturdays
he doesn't need to see me
to know that I am there
I am often in fear of what metaphor I am becoming to people
without my permission
"The most high-risk
homosexual behavior
I engage in
is
simply existing"

For Jackson Howard

It is only natural
to be misunderstood
and the irony is not lost on me
when we are both caught red-handed
guilty of the crime
of being faggots
that the world assumes
because I walk beside him
like he is my most valued possession
that he is my boyfriend
but does not a best friend
still smell as sweet?
I am never annoyed
that the world thinks
we belong to each other
because we do

he is my father
and my newborn
I take the greatest of care with him
when I rub the sleep from his eyes
rub his shoulders
pull the boogers from his nostrils

wipe the shimmer

from his starry eyelids

before we go back to the party

it is not hard to see

what they see

when we are together

the way our eyes soften

in each other's direction

hints at

the silent song we sing to each other

the vowels so clear they are invisible

sometimes even to us

but unlike

other faggots

who are best friends

we do not pretend that we are not in love

the magnetic string of Eros

that runs between us

so goddamn sharp

it could cut metal

or

stitch these two things in place

and I

hold his hand in public

not because I am the boy who is

slaying his box
but because
I am the boy
who's going to give him away
on his wedding day

In a Participatory Capitalism

I had convinced myself
that I should take a more active role
in de-escalating
my high-ass blood pressure
in terms of white powders
I am of the ilk
who will be done in
by sugar, salt, and flour
well before cocaine or ketamine
I convince myself
to go buy running shoes
I will only use
two weeks out of the year
four if I'm feeling it
but owning them
just feels responsible?
What is not so responsible
is the fact
that I have learned to love the self-inflicted public
    humiliation
of jogging in public
this stranger saw me jogging
or rather

attempting to

and ran up to ask me

"Sir, are you OK?"

'Cause in all reality people who jog in public

look FUCKED-UP

like

"what are they running from?"

Jogging in public

reads as

"I just want to be liked"

I do work on my body to attract members

of my same sex

when I could just as easily

pray for the courage

to die alone

like come the fuck on already

Sometimes, in the gossip columns

when they run the headlines that read

"list of celebrities that used to be hot but are all now FAT AS
    FUCK"

they praise the one

who eventually loses

the most weight

when the competition should actually be about

who served both looks the best

I have been 300 pounds
I have been 160 pounds
no matter what weight you start at
people always compliment
the loss of the first ten
"OMG!"
And
"wow!"
And
"good job!"
And "look at your effort!"
The loss of weight
and the compliments
are signifiers
that we are participating in capitalism
picking ourselves up by the bootstraps
taking control of the fact
that if our bodies are unpleasing to the eyes of the average
    stranger
it can only mean a moral deficit
on the hands of fatty

but also
how are we tracking the belief
that skinny people are actually happy?
When I was 160 pounds
it was jogging that got me there

but also
massive rails of cocaine
people said
"You look AMAZING"
it never occurred to me
that one can always respond
"Thank you, I'm suffering"
only one true friend took heed of this
and called me
"suspiciously skinny"
and the spell was broken
and I gained my weight again
and I am back to hell
I am jogging
around Lake Merritt
people are giving me the nod
of a participatory/social capitalism
nods that say
"We see that you are fat and trying—and worthy of our
    unsolicited praise"
I sink back into my body that sits
on these forever-aching knees
and it's always been apparent to me
that I have always existed
in
an expanding
and shrinking Universe

Diversity Hire

1.

I am fully fatigued by the #blackboymagic hashtag
but of course we know that the only thing worse
than a magical Negro
is an UN-magical Negro
honestly Hollywood deserves neither

I have come to the conclusion that
I owe you bitches nothing
I stay ashy
because ashy is natural
and I stay dehydrated
because water tastes boring to me
but also largely because of
how often I cry
I get disgusted
at how goddamn often they tell
the poets
to "put your pain in your work," that then your pain becomes
     immortal
and the work a sort of tombstone
but I don't refute *my life my life my life my life*

in the sunshine
and in the season of my ashy dehydrated life in the sun
people pretend to not understand
why I am insulted by being called thirsty by those who giggle
    over my corpse
with an extra glass of water
and a vitamin C pack in their hand
does nobody love me?
Water is free
like, it literally falls out of the sky
and California
is currently not in a drought
but to maintain a certain order
I stay dehydrated
who has the time these days to go to the bathroom every
    twenty minutes

my best friend
is the slacker white boy poet
who somehow also works for Hollywood
and makes three times the money I do
to be fair
he grew up
just as abused as I did
the only difference is
"My neoliberal parents taught me the coded language of

money. You are great at suffering—but you need more
   representation"
the thought of having to convince MORE people that I am
   worthy
of a six-figure salary
feels like, well, work
and also a sham
in all honesty, I am LITERALLY the lazy Black person white
   supremacy warned you about
"YAAAAAAAS QUEEN, GIVE US NOTHING!!!"

2.

The position of "staff writer"
so very suits the tagline of my life in that
"People LOVE being entertained by me—but no one ever
   actually does what the fuck I say."
Instead, I buy in to opt out
I'm going to sit in this room of white people, shut my Black-
   ass mouth, be well-behaved, groomed, collect this coin,
   and not let anyone know how demonically niggerish
I truly am
every once in a while
Hollywood pretends
that it wants to hear what I have to say

"I script Black boy MURDER" (she wrote)
but no one really wants to hear about me
and less often
actually wanna hear FROM ME at all
I try not to be the kind of extravagant human
who privileges
his triggers for trauma

I am unfairly triggered
most of the time.
This is no fault of my present company of course.
But
oh god
the flashbacks
of when I was a little faggot
talking to my stepdad or gym teacher or whoever else
thought that even my silence
was taking up too much space
"Oh god the little faggot, he's talking again—he thinks he has
    something to say—let's just smile and nod at him"
is no one listening to me or am I
just not talking?
I can't tell anymore

3.

I can say that I am an angry man
but also I am still a responsible citizen.
I try very hard not to make
the only six white people I engage with
on a weekly basis
a metaphor
for the greater percentage
that want me dead.
I don't tell anyone about it, the balancing act
'cause it's rude to admit
that you have no fucking clue
what is going on
or
how to push this void further away
I play the part
but I am no actor
only a scriptwriter
or at the very least
I try to *act* like one
though I hardly understand the assignment
or who they want me to become.
I know very little
about being a Black pimp
and more than I would like to know

about being a Black prostitute
every Hollywood writers' room
mirrors every other room full of people on Earth
we mutually engage
in a participatory capitalism of
"whose feelings are bigger"
and I have to opt out
as in
there is no gold medal to be had in the Oppression Olympics
I shut the fuck up more often than I dare explain myself
these fucking hoes out here can't even feel their own pain
like hell,
I should trust them with *mine*
I keep my Black boy bellyaching
confined to poems because I know
people are very threatened
by how competent I pretend to be

I expect them to expect me
to marry a white man
move to the Hudson Valley
and never complain about anything ever again
Blacks, Jews, white-passing people of any given racial group,
    and the invisible races (respectfully)—they all see me
I see the cold dismissive disdain
in virtually everyone's eyes

whenever I try to explain

that "token Negro"

is (unfortunately) not a resting position

but in the twilight of my salad days

I have grown to find comfort in people expecting

absolutely nothing out of me

I keep tabs on

who is bigger

at feeling nothing

and I guess the winner will be me today

and I can have you guess why it presently feels

like it is against the laws of physics

to feel pleasure right now

"I SCRIPT BLACK BOY MURDER" (she wrote)

Mood: Bored

I'm always being cheated out of a future
I once thought
was safe to believe in
I'm not even talking about important shit
like the threat of southern Colorado
one day becoming a coastal region
or even
the episodic rise and fall (and rise and fall)
of the right wing
I tend to only fatalistically worry about ignorant shit
like
soooooooooooooo stupid
you could call this fever of worry
"headless"
for instance how in the nineties
we spent days dreaming of videophones
until the day "we" (or like a team of scientists or whatever?
    I'm sure it was a collaborative effort? WHOEVER THE
    FUCK IT WAS . . .)
dreamed telephonic cameras
into existence
and that's when suddenly
none of my shitty bitch-face friends

wanted to answer the phone anymore
decided
that we actually would rather see less of people
that overnight
it became our civic duty
to answer this future prayer
that melted into a promise
that dissolved into a chore
that then wrapped its vicious racket
around our necks
of the extreme urge to noncommit

In everyone
tucked neatly
in an unsolicited face time
the world is chock-full of oaths
of civic promise
that if we think about it
we never fully agreed to
if at all
and by answering the phone
for unwanted conversation
we are somehow
fulfilling our end
of the cultural contract
as if we made

some unspoken deal with god
to always meet the future halfway
I
having no millennial fear
pick up
quite feverishly
no matter who is calling
like my life
codepended on it

AUNTIE

I am trying to be frugal
in feeling new media
nudging me
insisting that I talk shit about
my baby siblings
Auntie is too lazy
to judge and
I, for one, dig the new breed
but remain hesitant in this way
'cause like my cousin Juliana Huxtable once said
"The children are ashy and entitled"
and sometimes
much like their aunt,
unrealistic
and also,
but most importantly,
blessedly poor and
completely forgiven
for all trespasses

In the history of man
who can accurately recall
what group of twenty-year-olds

weren't raging assholes?
The old-timers pretend to forget
they were assholes too
and largely still are
my baby sister
loves me
despite the fact
I read like a crazy old slut to her
and I always thought she knew why I was crazy
why did I always assume
we had grown up
with the same eyes?
The day
she sheepishly disclosed
that she could not recall
ANYTHING
that happened in the house we grew up in
I cried uncontrollably, 'cause like,
oh, sweet sister
I'm not crazy
I was just the human fire wall
between you and
the great evil
of those headless fucking boomers
we called
Mom and Dad

The evil of our parents
and their parents
and their parents before that
we wear the mark of it
but I think this is true
(I have a world of younger siblings who are of no blood
    relation)
the young don't remember
and the old forget
and I wish to be an object sometimes
sometimes objectification is easier
for instance
I bike past the modern buildings in downtown
and ponder
the gentry
"It's so ugly and new. Burn it."
Yes. Of course.
But also,
it will outlive us all
and in a hundred years someone
will be fighting to save it

I move past the fever
of my first teaching
I pray
to find a way to slow down time

and relearn
how to actually breathe
properly apply my eyeliner and think
"steadfast"
Auntie (the old witch)
has to fight
until she dies

SEX (I'm a . . .)

I have taken to calling myself
"they" and "them"
for no other reason than
it's my goddamn business
it sounds
godlike
"they are going"
"they left"
my gender impressed
perfected
I'm abandoning that which does not serve me
(I feel like a total asshole typing this)
but perhaps my gender should have served me better?
If the world
actually intuited me as a man
why doesn't anyone
ever
actually do what the fuck I say?

These are the thoughts
I keep to myself
how often
we are all named
unreliable narrators of our own narrative

and is it not also crushing to remember
that "public image"
is NOT what we think of ourselves
but what others think of us
("may I have a crumb please, sir")
I am burning though
"them"
and even "they"
are leaving me
on an anatomical level I am breaking up
with everything
I remember
when I was twelve
the lady my babysitter smoked crack with
came over to the house and saw me sleeping on the couch
and asked "OMG, is that a girl?"
And with what trace amount of male pride I could muster
I became defeated I guess

that is until
twenty years later I was in the Castro
smoking crack
with someone who babysat me in my twenties
and they explained
"If you're a man who's never been asked, 'Are you a girl?' then
    you're probably just fucking UGLY"
oh how I twirled in those precarious years

when the term "she" was still
a gender-neutral term
"she is coming"
"she is going"
and like
we weren't even always talking about a person, mind you
every living object became feminine
"Who is she" we would say
at each new patron
entering
the Bar on Castro
and every so often some other bitch we couldn't stand would
     press through
and we were like
"I know who she IS
I just don't know who she THINKS she is"
then one day
we kinda gave up on that too

It was also around that time
I sat in an art lecture and became quite hot
(in a good way)
when the lady
lecturer concluded
"We could actually burn all the Picassos
to no great moral consequence"
and a singular white man in the audience

nearly shit his pants
and so the speaker continued
"I mean, do you understand how much sacred art
from how many countless cultures
has been burned?
At least there are pictures of the Picassos.
I think it would be
a great experiment to burn them."
And ah,
there
there was the thing
I was looking for
the notion that somehow
there is always room
or maybe we are always clearing the way
for the new
or
we are both in the process of becoming
and unbecoming
and have fully arrived or maybe
we don't need another hero
but surely I need not explain myself
for you to understand
why
on an anatomical level
I am breaking up with everything

Black Grrrls

I share
with female rappers
and
with the R&B singer grrrls
the crass predicament that if it wasn't for fuck niggas
I would be out of a career
(and when I say "fuck nigga" I mean myself included)
six albums later
I am still singing the blues
I am wearing
a white gardenia in my hair
and am contemplating the void
if not also what I will perform
for my third encore
I am gilded
canon
allow me to reintroduce myself
no side-eye of mine
will betray
the crown I wear

there is so little use
in ever trying to cancel

the queens of Urban radio
for I myself am living proof
that everyone loves
a Black girl with problems

"how do you make love to a drum machine?"

My light-skint boyfriend
ain't shit y'all
I have *begged* that nigga
to stop calling me
he thinks me rude for having said
"I'm too Black for you or anyone"
with his big-ass caramel candy bar colored dick in my mouth
he says that I
am just no good for him
when I am in fact the only one
bending over backward over the sheets
just to press him
I have begged him not to call me
and he still opens the door
when I show up
unannounced

My Jewish boyfriend
is a white boy y'all
he is a dizzying mix
of complete fucking nerd
and walking sex god
I get too lost

in his wire circular frames
and soft baby brown curls
AND: yes he lives in Brooklyn (of course)
AND: yes he gets lost in me all the time
he had me over a bench
in Tompkins park
eating my pussy
I recall him saying
"YOU. WILL. VOTE. BERNIE."
(And don't tell anybody, but I totally did)

My Mexican boyfriend
has PTSD
from surviving eighties Los Angeles
I got too comfortable one night
and hurt my baby's feelings
and he said
"California ain't big enough for the both of us right now"
but I got real hip
and ironed all my vintage Pendletons
made sure my fade was murderously edged
and surrendered my flower
every time he telepathically asked me to
after I was a good boy
he called me his "prized possession"
and said "Don't piss me the fuck off no more"

My Iranian boyfriend
was being hunted
he said he had spurned the wrong official
had sucked one too many dicks
(as we girls tend to do)
he said he had seventy-two hours to flee
or *surely* it was curtains
I was holding the version of him
that resided in the universe where he got to live
he was a celebrated photographer
and in a photo-essay
he painted the same word all over my body
that in Farsi
roughly translated to
"my temple"
and I just about
died

My Nigerian boyfriend
is the king
of my digital mailbox
he is insisting that I am
the most beautiful Black man
he's ever electronically seduced
and he should be the only honest judge
of what beautiful dark skin should be

'cause like, of course

and he says

"Fly me over and let's get married real quick"

and I'm down but also like

before I give him my credit card info

I humbly mutter to myself

"Mail-order brides are for, like, lonely desperate old
     American men"

which if I think about it . . .

Emotional/Content

Oh honey, you can hate me
to yr heart's content
until yr heart is content
I call myself an empath on the internet so I hold
a performative yet truly genuine
respectful
amount of space
for your feelings
for most people's feelings actually
but there are those two or three people from any given era
    of my life
at whom I actually have half a mind
while they are trashing me to my face
to flash my "only god can judge me" tattoo
that I had tatted on my Asshole
but it's just as easy to say
"Oh, my bad girl, I won't do it again"
I need not frown
upon my hilariously bad parenting
I live
in a social democracy
where someone
who grew up with better parenting

will emotionally beat my ass
if my cave-child self peaks in the red too much
this societal check and balance is foolproof
but I am still an American
which means I am rude
and have options
if I don't like you parenting me
with yr parents' style of punishment
I can take my apology back and kindly remind you that
"yo mama ain't shit
ya daddy ain't shit
and you ain't shit either, bitch"
I will not scream this at you
and because I am a romantic
I'll only say it with my eyes

Sociopath by Proxy

There really are men who think they are too good to pay
    for sex.
Incels decry a lack of pussy
when that three thousand dollars they spent
on video games
could have so easily been flipped into several nights
that they would remember
the rest of their no-stroke-game-havin'-ass life

I have easily
spent two hundred dollars
on dates where I didn't get laid
paying a hooker is the Lord's work
I am simply
cutting out the middleman
I promise you
and yes I could go dig deeply
through the dusty dingy thrift store that is Grindr
where if I wait long enough
eons even
someone I sorta wanna fuck will sorta wanna fuck me back
but I am a busy professional man
and time is money
and trains must run on time

I know in all forms of capitalism
both financial and emotional
money makes things move faster
I need everything to happen when the fuck I say so
and really
sometimes
we have to admit
radically
and honestly
that I am only technically handsome
but more so am generally too tired from work to be witty or
    charming all the time
so like generations upon generations upon generations
    of men
with my level of emotional fatigue
I turn to hookers

some men of my age pay for entire families
oh god
babies even
and some of these men are even poorer than me
I gave this younger man
two hundred bucks
'cause if I think about it
him slaying my box with that nine-inch pipe
is so easily worth the four bags of weed I can't afford anymore
I'm literally just as high after

'cause like you know
sex addiction . . . anyway

It is woven into the fabric of society that men
have to pay either financially
or emotionally to keep their dicks wet
I don't curse straight men for having illegitimate children
or
mistresses whose children's college tuition they pay
there are those of us who don't blame our forefathers
for being whoremongers
but admittedly only in the context that
their wives were over their dicks *years* ago
and don't wanna fuck them anymore
and Sally up the street
needs two hundred bucks
but maybe I am telling something too autobiographical
let me start again

every day of our lives
our masculine fatale
and oh-so-mythical sex drive
causes carnage
and equally is easily weaponized against us
I saw a bus ad in L.A. that said
"sexually risky?"
with a disembodied hand

tossing two dice

directly at me

no

this is not a fever dream

this is a *bus stop billboard*

this is as triggering for the sexually active

as it is for the person who has not been touched for years

whether we are having too much

too little

or even

god help us

a responsible amount

we pray that cognitive behavioral therapy

such as

and for instance

jerking off to porn with the sound on loud but the picture off

will return us to that first pure

godlike feeling we first have of sex but that long ago

became a logical body function as holy but as unceremonious

as breathing

or eating

or brushing our teeth

but there is no therapy on Earth I have found

that replaces

a big-ass Black dick (or medium-ass Black dick—if need be)

rubbing against my jiggly booty

we are all comically poisoned
I stole my uncle's
Cooleyhighharmony tape
when I was ten and heard
"sympin' ain't easy"
and was tickled when I learned that some straight men
call each other "simps"
for shit like
going to strip clubs
and putting money
in a stripper's pussy and believing
the girl actually likes you
but in a strip club context isn't that what you are paying for?
Pretending that a beautiful girl likes you is still a very beautiful
    feeling
and ostensibly not toxic if done in contained amounts
and as if desiring someone
that is only pretending to love you
were some form of insult we haven't all endured
or simply for the sake of argument
need be an insult at all

NEWEST ROMANTIC

I admit
that self-deprecation
is only a literary vehicle
"mostly only" that is
a relic I kept from my last ice age
I don't dare fully leave behind
because it was yet another rose I cultivated with great care
and it's mine

the world instills a certain self-hatred in us
and then takes that away too
why can't I ever own something that's mine?
We don't call them "disorders" anymore
we call them "adaptations" 'cause at some point in your life
walking with your head down was yes,
based in wanting to protect
your little heart,
but also
kept you from stepping blindly
into a pile of human shit someone left on the sidewalk
and that's good

These bad habits
that stuck to you like glue

at some indecipherable point in your life
kept you safe
and you held on to them like good-luck charms
but again
this was my last ice age
I'm thawing out
my self-esteem is flooding the Earth
I am coastal, yes,
but regionally speaking
all Americans are assholes
I am a rural Southerner
who has lived in California twenty years
which means I think the weather
is a perfectly acceptable topic of conversation
crucial even
and astrology intellectually
is mass bonding over a mutual love of folklore
people hate me just because I pretend to believe in astrology
I like believing in shit
there were even points in my life where I believed
FOR CERTAIN
that the Red Sea, at some point, did a standing ovation
I even recall it being
a very exciting thing to believe in
but I digress
god gave some men nine-inch dicks that actually work
    properly

100 percent of the time
or bank accounts filled by parents
that they did not have to pay for in blood
I can see it in your eyes that you can tell
I've had some form of very difficult life
you are wildly turned on
by the fact
that god gave me the bandwidth
to love and accept you
anonymously
and unconditionally
you are wildly turned on by me
because you know
I will suck your dick in the bathroom
sheerly for the camaraderie
or even because you asked nicely

I am a beautiful man
I am only forty
I could be your new husband
but I'm overqualified for the job

Golden Postures

"The Negro dance . . . is a rhythm of disintegration . . ."
said Martha Graham
and we all know
the alcoholic white modernists
of last century
were oracles and
how I wish it weren't true
(the disintegration part)
and yes I often find it hard to find equilibrium
and my arabesque
lacks a certain poetic quality
though I do not self-deprecate
or need remind myself
that god made all of this
I am still sculpture
and consider
I was a man of forty before I danced in pointe shoes
heard the ballet teacher say
"Let the weight hang off you and on your ankles like your
    pelvis is lifted on a silver tray and like your head is hovering
    with the weight of a celestial crown or so help me, your
    neck from a noose"

I give the illusion of floating
when I'm in free fall
from the vantage point of the audience
I look like I'm flying
but from this vantage point of me
passed out on the floor
looking
upside down
what could not be imagined
or dreamed into existence

I sometimes mistake streetlights
for the moon
or a stage light
as epiphany
like the Hanged Man I am Major Arcana
I hang myself out of a self-inflicted predicament
I see the world from a new perspective
and don't cry for me when you see me on the floor
I am basking in
my celestialness
would you believe
that I am happy?

Every day
the scorched me reintegrates

and learns how to talk and walk again and again and again
and over and over
it's all episodic
two nooses pull me
from my crown and my foot
it's giving erect posture
and I've nothing to fear
for I am held together by spine and not glue
I do this dance every goddamn day
my golden posture
remains earned

Neurodivergence vs. "Moral Deficit": Defined

As an adult sufferer of ADHD
I can only beg you to believe me
when I tell you about the amount of emotional battering
I take
at the hands of people
who treat me
like a neurological teapot
that has to be attended to
every time I shriek with steam.
When I go on trips with friends
they especially make sure I don't buy the drugs
a few are also surprised
that I can do ANYTHING
they say shit like
"OMG! You have an Amazon account?! Did someone
    help you?!"
And I get it
I've not been very protective of my public image
I've had a very public bout
with composure in the face of time
it's proven
that repeated failure at a task

causes brain failure
it is a surprise
that I have enough brain function *left* to
spread my butt cheeks
and wipe my ass in sequential order
considering how much I have failed in life
at starting on time
leaving on time
or finishing
like, ever

what we used to call
poor parenting
is now called
neurodivergence
but since my brain still came
from my parents
I'm going to take the liberty of blaming
those broke (though well-meaning) motherfuckers
for ANY discomfort I feel from now into my last breath on
    Earth
you could say
I'm a self-centered narcissist
who shows up late
but this is not just moral deficit
I am conjuring alchemy

my misplaced belief
is that if I refuse to start
or go
or finish
I am somehow slowing down time itself
one thing I know
is two for certain:
I may not have a future
but I SURE AS FUCK have a present
it's always another light switch
I fear I did not turn off
or the gas
I find myself reclosing windows
that I should be jumping out of
as if Freddy Krueger is after me
which would actually be the only way to get me to leave the
    house
and sometimes
it's just fucking easier to ditch
those day-drinking brunch degenerates
I call friends
and stay my ass home
but I always just show up late
because prayer and practice are the only ways to master
deep deep flaws
I have taken to a new habit

of leaving just one minute earlier than the last time and two
    minutes before the time before last
and one day years from now
I might actually show up early

Daddy

I am a bastard and I'm through
I am so very over it
and am balancing on the precipice
of my fast-hardening arteries
and erectile dysfunction
NOW the boys start to flock to me
want to keep me warm at night
want to hear
what wisdom
I have scribed on a scroll:

Dear boys
I still don't know goddamn anything
or maybe only one thing for certain:
that is
being born with a dick
does not make you a man
there're more rules to it than that
like soooooooooooooo
many many many more
and as a man the only real path to peace
is that you must shut the fuck up
often

and with vigor
but keep in your back pocket the knowledge
of how to kill a son of a bitch
if need be
I have murdered myself in small amounts
so often
I've become ectoplasmic, can walk through walls

In my twenties
in San Francisco
when me and the other boys were in between father figures
we sometimes
had to be fathers for each other
The Lost Boys
I don't think I'll ever have that again
it was electric
in present day I come home
hopped up on amphetamines
and try to watch porn
I see sometimes
the dead boys
the ones I fathered
and the ones who fathered me
live on as porn puppies on the internet
"Cum Pigs Volume 3" and so on
I'm reminded of the fact

that most of the stars we see in the sky
are presumably dead
before their light reaches us
and the boy I called father will be immortalized
as the bottom getting fucked
in some anonymous stairwell
south of Folsom
I shouldn't have to explain to you
that when I say
"I feel old"
I'm not always talking about my body
sometimes I just mean
that my pussy feels old
and that my light isn't reaching another galaxy
fast enough
or will ever even do so
in my lifetime
which by current metrics is conceptually half over

I am often reminded
by men
only five or ten years older than me
that I still have a baby face
and that my gentrification of the term "old man" is an insult
to the decade they have on me
how blind the older men are

to their own lives
and mine
it need not take years of wisdom
to see that
I am a man
who is disappearing
and on a molecular level
my Black is cracking

I Am Decided

I said

to my gay uncle when I was twenty

"The boys don't like me"

not even looking up

from the fried chicken he was breading for dinner

he said to me

"Honey, go look outside that window there and on the
      sidewalk. You'll see that in San Francisco, even the trash
      gets picked up once a week"

Inevitables

Maybe one day
one of my books
will make it to hardback: covered
though maybe fitting
that they never are
I am usually
underdressed
and my thoughts
are very very naked
please do not let the nudity of my words
conjure any feelings
of seduction
theater taught me that
nudity need not represent sex
but rather, simplicity
or truth
and (perhaps most frequently)
protest
I am the single handsome father
of words
that do not belong to me
they don't even
belong

to themselves
and are only asking
very politely
for space to breathe
please
do not call me by my name
in fact
don't call me fucking ever

I might be the enemy they speak of.

IN LOVE

I am reaching a fevered pitch
I am making space
in my drafty and sparse museum
for a new arrival
a wingless Erotes, a bleached marble bust
that turns every color at once
each time
you pass by
and give it a kiss
and with each bleached marble kiss
I hear him say
the same prayer:
"I will suck you so far into the void, you will never ever see the
    light again"

. . . with no particular place to go / "no side to fall in"

"There is no faster way to get there"
I felt the remark unfortunate
despite the fact that I
was in no real hurry and that
I'm the one who said it
I miss Northern California when I leave it too long
you have to be there to actually notice it
all of California
tends to flatten in pictures
the endless depth
of the ridges and valleys doesn't translate
into the two-dimensionality of pictures
but on the flip side
L.A. bus doors open

I am not kicking both doors open
I'm taking a cab
when confronted with Los Angeles
as a map or grid
I hallucinate
a certain order
but in practice I have sat for forty-five minutes in this car

and am thinking what if all maps
are a bunch of little nowheres
all put together
and at this moment I find a certain peace in that
nonlocality
whether in a cab
or on my broomstick
I'll always fly away
'cause some nights
I don't want any of you motherfuckers finding me
but the other nights
most nights
I am always en route to another party
I will quickly run out of early
in certain contexts I love a party
of a thousand "hellos"
and saying goodbye (it's such a sad word ☹)
and flinging my little soul
as many places on the city grid map
as I can in a night

I am still flesh and bone
and no longer a party boy
but still make it a practice to haunt places
hope my soul
is making some kind of cosmic imprint

every time I lock eyes
with any given ten people
you may not be my type but I will still stop
to flirt
because even though you are not my type
you are still easily one of the most beautiful things
I've ever seen.

I take great pleasure
in seeing this not-ill-fated cab ride
as the pencil
making a connect-the-dots
of all the places I left soul stuff behind
and what infinite number of constellations could be imagined
all between

CUPID + Venus

Impressively disappointing
as it were
there was no one coming to save her
even if they had
the thrashing would have drowned
even her savior
"It was the fatigue"
he thought
the constant becoming
the fact that
every second was the future
the opening night was always just that
to his left
a forty-year-old performance artist
looked oxygenless
from the front of the stage she reminded him
before the house opened
"you saw the old whores who HAD to keep dancing"
and every day
we are no more weary
but more importantly
no more wounded

we know that we
coexist with trauma
it very easily
becomes unremarkable: our pain
the disturbances
and the tears and hairline fractures become so regular
like ticking clocks
"you saw the old whores who had to keep dancing"
and sometimes it seems the more I get fucked
or fingered ("triggered")
the wetter
and more receptive
I become

NORTHERN CALIFORNIA

1.

I wanted radical Glamour
with a capital *G*
we've stayed in the house so long we now seem unglamorous
and please let me extend this act
of reckless generosity
and kidnap you
to North Beach
and stuff your face with a hundred dollars' worth
of deep-fried
Cantonese
salt-and-pepper crab
no like
two hundred bucks' worth
we'll even get the champagne
and forty oysters
it's a beautiful life
oh oh oh oh

I just want to be here beside you
have been beside you
have always been by your side

North Beach was not new to us
I remember in 2006
when I was mopping jizz
at the Lusty Lady
and how after that horrible shift one night I met you
at the poetry reading
at City Lights Books
we found a bag of cocaine on the floor
(and we thought poets only drank)
we huffed that bag down
in like three seconds
and went racing through the store
and snuck into where we were certainly not supposed to be
and you almost stole
the entire box labeled
"Ferlinghetti: archive of unpublished journals—
1968–1982"
and I said
"But Marcos, this is deplorably wrong?"
And we
COULDN'T
STOP
LAUGHING
after you said
"But, like, no one's even reading it!"

2.

The stop-start freeze-frame
kaleidoscopic density
of many lives packed into one
I have to
think of time in different ways
lest it consume me
but also
the line between
the past and the present
I have altogether abandoned
keeping score of
it's godlike
the poetic practice
of shrinking twenty years
into a series of days

Monday: I was born
Tuesday: I stepped off BART and into the San Francisco air the
    first time
Wednesday: the day I asked you to marry me and you refused
Thursday: the day you never woke up—I called and called
Friday: I became immortal because I wanted to remember
    forever

3.

Big Sur: we thought if we escaped for a day
things would feel better
but the winding highway gave us car sickness
and the epic cliffs reminded me
I'm acutely afraid of heights
and Highway 5 is sinking.
In undergrad
at California State East Bay
my geography teacher said
"Well by definition anything by the water is eroding—the
    whole thing will fall into the ocean in a hundred years"
I am drawn to anything that has finality
my own Dionysian caterwauling
now sounded like death bells
I had coexisted with so long
they now seemed like the humming of a car engine
navigating this highway—I'm reading the map
the driver is a handsome porn director
escaping a marriage
and I was cross at the world
'cause no one had asked to marry me
two harmonious opposites
I remember stopping
because the road got so violently curvy

I had to puke
we stopped and climbed to the foot
of a sort of bluff called "Jigsaw Junction"
before deciding to go home
if California is falling into the ocean
a couple of inches
each hundred years
then certainly we had enough time
to go home
and die peacefully

Self-Checkout

You already did the double take
got an extra glance
quite by mistake
but while I got you looking
you might as well take
the whole eyeful
until I become something
something that you own

Mature Gracefully

I'm tired of
pretending to care
about being sexy
I fucked up
my entire twenties
and thirties
with this overly utopic goal
this bullshit
has gone on long enough
I have reached deep inside myself
and found the courage
to be
ugly
old
and
defiantly unwantable
and the rest of you bitches
just
HAVEN'T
Tsk, tsk

Graduation / Death of Athenian Youth

I stand too easily
in between two points:
that which has yet to be reconciled
and that which is irreconcilable

the pondering of self
is of itself
religious rite
we call it "the mysteries"
not always because it is that which
cannot be named
but a certain time stamp:
"that which has no real conclusion"

my mother, grandmother, my Muh' Dear, and so on in their
    youth sang
"I believe I'll pray on—see what the end's gonna be"
but I defy my time-fearing matriarchs
I blaspheme:
I am the only real god
and if I sit so on high
privy: all time that has ever existed is visible
or

"that which has no real beginning"
for you can always pinpoint
any given genesis
and think
"but what happened before"
when I say "I am the only real god"
what I mean is "I am the only witness to who lives in this
    body"
it's perhaps godlike
to say
if all space became one building
and all of time, one second
and we annihilate the straight line
and only privilege the intersection
where the dimensions cross
it becomes
"you were never not born, and you were never not dead"
this is not "the answer"
this is the graveyard where it all falls apart

"linearity is not the hallmark of intersectionality"
we privilege the straight line
as the fastest route between two points
we watch too much TV
and have internalized that all things must have a linear
    message

bending to some form of status quo
but the intersections
with their wormholes, black holes, conflicted moralities,
    divine paradox
here—the poetic laws of physics dissolve
sweet sweet black hole that I am
I make my home here
and to dazzling effect
forgive me
for being too grand
but allow me, just for once in my life
to say
if all space became one building (my body)
and all time, one second (my lifetime)
it could stand to reason

"I am the only god here; I am the only witness to this body"

I have learned to love the hundred pounds
I have gained over the last two years
for no other reason than
I viscerally feel the effects of gravity more
the wave of invisible attraction
to the Earth
becomes more evident the heavier I become
either in body

or mind
and however idly I have spent
these forty years
and then
the next forty
the forty after that
simultaneously dulled
though no worse for wear
in this flash of a second
I am still raw

French Song . . .

J'avais entendu le son exploser

Deux chocs

L'un après l'autre

Sismiques

Je t'avais attendu toute la nuit dans la chambre d'hôtel

Je voulais récupérer la mixtape que je t'avais faite

J'avais volé jusqu'ici pour la récupérer

Je t'avais dit que je détestais la Californie

Je t'avais dit que je ne voulais pas rester longtemps

Tout au long du trajet qui nous sépare

J'ai laissé des petits mots

Semé des indices

Rouler des pelles ici et là

Des petits cailloux

Tu ne feras pas croire

Que t'as pas assez la dalle

Pour mordre à l'hameçon

T'es à moi

Tes émotions sont à moi

Je peux te faire aimer

Et

Je peux te faire haïr

Je te vois

Crever d'envie

De caresser

La peau de mon ventre

Dans ta tête

Je te vois t'imaginer

Frotter ton nez contre

Sans y mettre d'ego

C'est

La meilleure bite

Que t'as jamais eu, pas vrai?

J'entends la pluie tomber dehors, plus fort que la veille

Peut-être

Ironiquement

Parce que t'es mort de soif.

I had heard the tune blast

Two explosions

Side by side

Seismic

I had waited for you all night in the hotel room

I wanted the mixtape I made you back

I flew all the way here to get it

I told you that I hated California

I told you I would not be staying long

All across the space between me and you

I had left little notes

Hints

A tongue kiss here and there

Like little bread crumbs

Please do not pretend

You are not hungry enough

To take the bait

I own you

I own your emotions

I can make you love

And

I can make you hate

I see you

Dying

To touch

The skin on my stomach

Inside your head

I can see you see yourself

Rub your nose against it

I say with very little ego

That this

Is some of the best dick

You have ever had in your life, yes?

I hear the sound of rain outside much louder than yesterday

Perhaps

Ironically

Because you are very very thirsty

Eulogy

The encyclopedia
of my scandals
and failures
will always be
a more substantial read
than the pamphlet of your success
I bet money, bitch
on who will ring immortal

I will echo with reverb

Acknowledgments

I would like to thank the Alabama public school system for gifting me irony, foreshadowing, rage, and the secular witchcraft that is literature. And also my eighth-grade writing teacher, the rabbi's wife, who gifted me banned literature.